# TREES

# TREES

*An Anthology of*
*Writings and Paintings*
*by*

# HERMANN
# HESSE

*Selected by*
Volker Michels

*Translated by*
Damion Searls

KALES
PRESS

*Kenneth Kales*, Editor
*Bonnie Thompson*, Associate Editor
*Sarah Bowen*, Assistant Editor
Cover design by *Laura Klynstra*
Book design by *Leah Carlson-Stanisic*

All rights reserved.
Library of Congress Cataloging-in-Publication Data
Names: Hesse, Hermann, 1877–1962, author. | Michels, Volker, editor. |
Searls, Damion, translator.
Title: Trees / Hermann Hesse ; selected by Volker Michels ; translated by
Damion Searls.
Other titles: Bäume. English
Description: First edition. | San Diego, California : Kales Press, [2022] |
Series: Lacinato ; book 1 | Summary: "A collection of Mr. Hesse's poems,
essays, and extracts on trees accompanied by an assemblage of his
paintings"—Provided by publisher.
Identifiers: LCCN 2021062011 (print) | LCCN 2021062012 (ebook) |
ISBN 9781737832713 (hardcover) | ISBN 9781737832720 (ebook)
Subjects: LCGFT: Poetry. | Essays. | Excerpts.
Classification: LCC PT2617.E85 B3813 2022 (print) | LCC PT2617.E85
(ebook) | DDC 838/.91209--dc23/eng/20220124
LC record available at https://lccn.loc.gov/2021062011
LC ebook record available at https://lccn.loc.gov/2021062012

FIRST EDITION

Printed in Canada

ISBN-13: 978-1-7378327-1-3 print edition

ISBN-13: 978-1-7378327-2-0 ebook edition

kalespress.com

San Diego, California

# CONTENTS

* Titles followed by an asterisk were supplied by the German editor,
Volker Michels, for untitled poems or excerpts from longer works.

PLATE 1

# TREES

Trees, for me, have always been the most compelling preachers. I worship and adore them when they live in families and tribes, in forests and groves—and even more when they stand alone. They are like solitary people. Not hermits who've stolen away from society out of some weakness, but great, lonely people, like Beethoven or Nietzsche. The world rustles in their uppermost branches, their roots rest in the infinite, but they do not lose themselves in either, they work with all the strength of their lives toward just one thing: fulfilling their own law that lives within them, shaping their own form, becoming their own selves. Nothing is more sacred, nothing more exemplary, than a strong and beautiful tree.

When a tree is cut down and shows its fatal wound naked to the sunlight, we can read its whole history in the bright disk of its trunk and gravestone: in its annual rings and deformities are faithfully recorded all the struggle, all the suffering and illness, all the joy and flourishing, the lean years and rich years, attacks withstood and storms outlasted. And every farm boy knows that the hardest, noblest wood has the narrowest rings, and that the most indestructible, strongest, most exemplary trunks grow high in the mountains, in constant danger.

Trees are holy. If you know how to talk to them, how to listen to them, you will learn the truth. They preach not doctrines and rules: they preach, with no concern for details, the primal law of life.

A tree says: Hidden in me is a seed, a spark, a thought. I am life from eternal Life. The attempt the eternal Mother made with me, the risk She took, is unique—my shape is unique, the grain of my skin, the tiniest play of leaves on my crown and the tiniest scar on my bark. My task is to give shape to the eternal, and to show that shape in its unique, distinctive particularity.

A tree says: My power is trust. I know nothing about my fathers, I know nothing about the thousand children I produce every year. I live out the mystery of my seed to the very end— that is my only concern. I trust that God is within me. I trust that my task is a holy one. I live from this trust.

When we're sad and have difficulty enduring our life any longer, a tree can say to us: Be quiet! Be at peace! Look at me! Life is not easy, nor is it hard. Those are childish thoughts. Let God speak within you while you stay silent. You are scared because your path is leading you away from your mother and your home. But home is not here or there. Home is inside you, or else it is nowhere.

A fierce desire to wander and roam tugs at my heart when I hear the trees rustling in the evening wind. If you listen long and closely, this longing to travel, too, reveals its seed, its meaning. It is not, as it seems, a longing to run away from your sorrows. It is a longing for home, for the memory of your mother, for new images and parables for life. It leads you back home. Every path leads home, every step is a birth, every step is a death, every grave is the mother.

That is how the tree rustles in the evening, when our own childish thoughts are scaring us. Trees have long thoughts—drawn out, calm, long of breath—the same way they have longer lives than we do. They are wiser than we are, at least than we are when we do not heed them. But once we've learned how to listen to the trees, the brevity and speed and childish haste of our thoughts attain a gladness without equal. Those who have learned to listen to trees no longer want to be a tree. They do not yearn to be anything but what they are. That is home. And that is happiness.

PLATE 2

# MY HEART GREETS YOU

My heart greets you, oh faithful trees,
Still tall and strong like you were before,
When I concealed my first young dreams
Of love inside your night.

I hear within your leaves the whisper
Of songs I sang when I was young,
Songs that would twin themselves with the moonlight,
Timid and shy in the light of day.

I greet you too, you timid songs,
Reminding me of better times
When delighted by rose and lilac I tied
A first bouquet for my darling.

Your seductive sound so sweet, unique
To you, like the new green of tender spring,
When the first larks full of pleasure fly
Above newly awakened branches.

What I have sung since those bygone times
Was not so sweet, not so unique,
It only echoed, painfully,
The sound and light of my first love.

# GOOD FRIDAY

An overcast day, still snow in the woods,
The blackbird sings among bare branches:
Brandishing shyly the breath of spring,
Swollen with lust, aggrieved with woe.

Tight-lipped and tiny in the grass
The crocus folk, the violet bed
Smells timidly of it knows not what,
It smells of death and of festival.

The buds on the trees are blind with tears,
The sky hanging low, so close, so anxious,
And all the gardens, all the hills,
Are Gethsemane and Golgotha.

PLATE 3

Dieses Blatt zu katharinas Geburtstag am 6.3.1984 von
Heiner

2.8. IV. grün-dünnsten 19 13 ?

**PLATE 4**

# THE OLD COPPER BEECH

I t was a moderately large park, not very wide but deep, with stately elm, maple, and plane trees, winding paths to stroll along, a copse of young fir trees, and lots of benches to sit and rest on. Amid all this were bright sunny lawns, some empty, some adorned with circular flower beds or ornamental shrubbery, and there in the warm and cheerful freedom of the grass, conspicuous and alone, stood two large individual trees.

One was a weeping willow. A narrow lathwork bench circled its trunk, and the tree's long delicate silky tired branches hung so dense and deep all around that being inside them was to be in a tent or temple, where despite the eternal shade and twilight a muted constant warmth brooded.

The other tree, separated from the willow by a meadow with a low fence, was a mighty copper beech. From a distance it looked dark brown, almost black. But when you got closer, or stood under it and looked up, all the leaves on the outer branches, penetrated by the sunlight, burned with a low warm purple fire shining with a solemnly subdued glow like a church's stained-glass windows. This old copper beech was the most well-known and remarkable beauty in the park, visible from every direction. It stood dark and alone in the middle of the bright grassy landscape, and it was tall enough that when you looked at it from anywhere in the park you would see its firm, round, beautifully domed crown in the middle of empty blue sky, and the brighter and more dazzling the blue was, the blacker and more solemn the treetop resting in it. It looked very different depending on the weather and time of day. You would often feel when looking at it that it knew how beautiful it was, and that it stood proud and alone, far from the other trees, not without reason. It swaggered; it looked coolly out at the sky, looked past and over everything. It also often seemed well aware that it was the only tree of its kind in the garden, that it had no brothers. Then it would look across to the other, distant trees, searching, yearning. It was most beautiful in the morning, and also in the evening until the sun turned red, but then suddenly it was almost like it was extinguished, and night seemed to come to the place where it stood an hour earlier than to everywhere else. It looked darkest and strangest on rainy days. While the other trees breathed, and stretched, and happily flaunted their brighter greens, it stood in its solitude as if dead, black from the treetop down to the ground. It didn't shiver but you could tell it was freezing, and that it was uncomfortable and ashamed, standing there exposed and alone.

At one time, the regularly laid out pleasure garden had been a rigorous work of art. But a time came when people grew tired of arduous waiting and tending and pruning, and no one cared about laboriously planted grounds, and the trees were left to fend for themselves. They had struck up friendships with one another, they had forgotten their artificially isolated roles, they had remembered in their crisis their old forest homeland, leaned on one another, flung their arms around one another for support. They had covered the paths straight as arrows with thick foliage and drawn those paths to themselves, with their long, grasping roots, transforming them into nourishing forest floor; their crowns had clasped one another and grown tightly intertwined; and they saw an eagerly upward-striving population of new trees grow under their protection, filling the emptiness with smoother trunks and lighter-colored leaves, conquering the fallow soil, making the earth black and soft and rich with their shade and fallen leaves, so that mosses and grass could now thrive more easily too, and little shrubs.

By the time still other people came and wanted to use the former gardens for leisure and pleasure once more, they had turned into a little forest. It had to be cut back. The old path between the plane trees was restored, but other than that, these people were content to make narrow, winding footpaths through the thicket, sow the heather-covered clearings with grass, and set up green benches in good places to sit. And the people whose grandfathers had planted the plane trees in ramrod-straight lines, and pruned and shaped them with judgment and discretion, now visited those trees with their own children and were happy that the long period of desolation had turned the allées into a forest, where sun and wind could linger and birds could sing and people could indulge in their thoughts and dreams and desires.

## MOVEMENT AND STILLNESS
## IN HARMONY

When we were still in our dry spring, before a run of stormy days and rains, I would often go to a spot in my vineyard where at the time I had my campfire somewhere the garden's soil hadn't yet been dug up. In the middle of the whitethorn hedge that defines the border of the garden, a beech tree grew up years ago. At first it was a little shrub from a seed flown over from the woods, but for several years I let it stay there, just for the time being, somewhat against my will. (I felt bad for the whitethorn.) Then the delicate little winter beech prospered so prettily that I accepted it once and for all, and now it has already become a nice thick little tree, and I am twice as fond of it because the old mighty beech that was my favorite tree in the whole nearby woods has been recently cut down. Massive segments of its trunk, sawn apart, still lie there heavy and oversized like rubble from an ancient column. My little tree is probably a child of that beech.

PLATE 5

It always delighted and impressed me how stubbornly my little beech held on to its leaves. When everything else was long since bare, it still stood clad in its withered leaves—through December, January, February; storms tore at it, snow fell on it and dripped off again, and the dry leaves, at first dark brown, grew ever paler, thinner, silkier, but still the tree would not let them go, they were needed to shield the young buds. Then at some point or another every spring—and every time it was later than you expected—the tree would one day have changed. It would have lost its old foliage and instead put out tender new buds dabbed with moisture. This time, I was witness to the transformation. It was an afternoon hour around mid-April, soon after the rain had made the landscape fresh and green; I had still not heard the cuckoo that year, not seen any daffodils in the meadow. Only a few days earlier I had stood there in a hard north wind, shivering, raising my collar, and watched with amazement as the beech stood indifferent in the wrenching wind, dropping barely a leaf. Tough and brave, hard and stubborn, it kept hold of its old bleached leaves.

And now, today, as I broke pieces of wood by my fire in the gentle calm warm air, I saw it happen: a soft breeze blew up, just a breath really, and the leaves saved for so long simply drifted off, by the hundreds and thousands—noiselessly, easily, willingly, tired from their long perseverance, tired of their stubbornness and fortitude. What had resisted and endured for five or six months now succumbed to a puff of air, a nothing, because the time had come and their furious persistence was no longer needed. Away they flew and fluttered, smiling, without a struggle, ready. The tiny wind was much too weak to carry the little leaves far no matter how light and thin they were, so they drizzled down like a light rain and covered the path and the grass at the foot of the little tree, which was now showing a few buds already broken open and green.

What had this surprising and touching performance revealed to me? Was it death: the easy, willingly undergone death of the winter leaves? Was it life: the urgently striving, celebratory youth of the buds making space for themselves with a suddenly roused will? Was the performance sad or cheering? Was it a sign that I, an old man, should let myself flutter and fall as well, a warning that I might be taking up space needed by the younger and stronger? Or was it a call to hold on, like the beech leaves—to stay on my feet and brace myself and defend myself as tenaciously and as long as I could, because then, at the right moment, my farewell would be easy, serene, and joyful? No, like everything we see it was the great and eternal made visible: a confluence of opposites, their fusing together in the fire of reality. It meant nothing, was a call to nothing; or, rather, it meant everything—it meant the mystery of existence and it was beautiful, it was happiness and meaning, a gift and a discovery for anyone who saw it, like an earful of Bach or an eyeful of Cézanne. These names and these interpretations were not part of the experience, they came later: the experience itself was nothing but appearance, miracle, mystery, as beautiful as it was serious, as fair and propitious as it was unrelenting and merciless.

At the same place, by the whitethorn hedge near the beech, on one of those balmy, humid, changeable, windswept stormy days already preparing the leap from spring into summer, when the world had meanwhile turned succulent and green and the first cuckoo's cry had sounded in our woods on Easter Sunday, the great mystery spoke to me again in the form of a visual experience that was no less symbolic. The great theater of the clouds was performing in a sky at once overcast and still flinging blinding glimpses of sunlight down into the valley's germinating green. The wind seemed to be blowing from all directions, although south-to-north seemed to predominate. The atmosphere was at high tension, filled with restless passion. And in the middle of this play, suddenly demanding I look at it, stood another tree: a young and beautiful tree, a freshly leaved poplar in the neighbor's garden. It shot up like a rocket, waving back and forth, elastic, sharply pointed, stiffly compacted like a cypress in the short breaks in the wind, and gesturing as the wind picked up again with a hundred thin branches combed into separate strands. The top of this magnificent tree rocked back and forth, reared up with delicately flashing, whispering leaves, delighting in its power and green youth, swaying slightly but meaningfully like the needle on a balance, now yielding in a game of flirtatious teasing, now springing willfully back straight.

(Only later did I remember that I had already observed this game before, decades ago, with my senses open, and had portrayed it in a poem called "Flowering Branch.")

# FLOWERING BRANCH

Constantly this way and that
The flowering branch flails in the wind,
Constantly up and down
My heart flails like a child
Between bright days and dark,
Between wanting and renouncing.

Until the flowers have blown away
And the branch is covered in fruit;
Until the heart, sated with childhood,
Has its rest
And confesses: it was full of pleasure, not for nothing,
This restless game of life.

PLATE 6

# THE MIRACLE OF REBIRTH

For the past few days the distant brown woods have cheerfully shimmered with fresh young green; today on the footbridge I found the first half-opened primrose blossoms; the gentle April clouds are dreaming in the wet clear sky, and the wide fields, barely plowed, are so dazzlingly brown, stretching out in the lukewarm air with such yearning that it is as if they long to receive, and sprout, and test and feel and squander their wordless powers in a thousand green seeds and upward-striving blades.

Everything waits, everything's preparing itself, everything dreams and springs—the seed up toward the sun, the cloud to the field, the young grass into the air—in a delicate, sweetly urgent fever of becoming. Year after year I wait for this time with impatience and longing, as though one special moment had to come that would unlock the miracle of rebirth for me, as though someday it simply had to happen that I would fully see and grasp and experience for one long moment the epiphany of power and beauty, how life leaps laughing from the earth and large young eyes open to the light. And then, year after year, the sound and scent of the miracle happen around me—loved and longed for and . . . not understood. Here it is, and I didn't see it coming, didn't see the seed crack open or the first tender spring water tremble into the light. All of a sudden there are flowers everywhere, trees shine with pale leaves or a lather of white blossoms, and birds hurtle joyously in beautiful arcs through the warm blue sky. The miracle has taken place, whether I saw it or not—forests arch overhead, distant peaks call, and it is time to take up one's boots and bag, oar and fishing pole, and delight with all one's senses in the young year more beautiful than ever before, just like it is every year, and which seems to be forging ahead in even more of a hurry every time. How long a spring used to be, how inexhaustibly long, back when I was a boy!

And when the hour permits it and my heart is of good cheer, I lie down and stretch out in the wet grass, or clamber up the nearest thick tree trunk, smell the perfume of the buds and the fresh resin, see the net of twigs and branches and the green and blue in a tangle over my head, and sleepwalk as a silent visitor into the sacred grove of my childhood. It so rarely happens, and is so precious when it does: vaulting over to the other side for once, breathing the clear morning air of first youth, and seeing the world once more, for a moment, as it came from God's hands—as we all saw it when we were children, when the miracle of strength and beauty was unfolding within ourselves.

Back then the trees rose so joyful and assertive into the air; the daffodils and hyacinths sprouted up in the grass so splendid and lovely; and the people—we knew so few back then—greeted us with affection and good wishes, for they could still sense on our shining brow the breath of the divine, which we ourselves had no idea was there, and which, unintended by and unbeknownst to us, would leave us under the pressure of growing up. What a wild and untamed boy I was, how much my father worried about me ever since I was little, how many fears and sighs I caused my mother! And yet God's brilliance shone from my brow, and whatever I looked at was beautiful and alive, and in my thoughts and dreams, even when they were anything but pious, miracles and angels and fairy tales came and went freely like brothers and sisters.

# SPRING NIGHT

Sleepily the wind reaches its feathers
Into the chestnut tree;
Down the pointed rooftops run
The twilight and light of the moon.

All the fountains coldly murmur
Muddled legends to themselves;
The ten o'clock bells, in their frames,
Solemnly prepare to toll.

In the gardens, heard by no one,
Trees shining in the moonlight slumber;
Through the depths of their round crowns rustle
The breaths of beautiful dreams.

I hesitantly put aside
My fiddle, grown warm with playing,
Stare in wonder far into the blue land
And dream and yearn and say nothing.

PLATE 7

# CHESTNUT TREES

verywhere we've lived takes on a certain shape in our memory only some time after we leave it. Then it becomes a picture that will remain unchanged. As long as we're there, with the whole place before our eyes, we see the accidental and the essential emphasized almost equally; only later are secondary matters snuffed out, our memory preserving only what's worth preserving. If that weren't true, how could we look back over even a year of our life without vertigo and terror!

Many things make up the picture a place leaves behind for us—waters, rocks, roofs, squares—but for me, it is most of all trees. They are not only beautiful and lovable in their own right, representing the innocence of nature and a contrast to people, who express themselves in buildings and other structures—they are also revealing: we can learn much from them about the age and type of arable land there, the climate, the weather, and the minds of the people. I don't know how the village where I now live will present itself to my mind's eye later, but I cannot imagine that it will be without poplars, any more than I can picture Lake Garda without olive trees or Tuscany without cypresses. Other places are unthinkable to me without their lindens, or their nut trees, and two or three are

PLATE 8

recognizable and remarkable by virtue of having no trees there at all.

Yet a city or landscape with no predominating woods of any kind never entirely becomes a picture in my mind; it always remains somewhat without character, to my feeling. There is one such city I know well—I lived there as a boy for two years—and despite all my memories of the place, my image of it is of somewhere foreign and alien; it has turned into a place as arbitrary and meaningless to me as a train station.

It's been a very long time since I've seen a real chestnut-tree city—this thought occurs to me whenever I see a single beautiful horse-chestnut tree around here or sadly catch sight of the shabby little horticultural chestnut trees in certain villages. If they only knew how chestnut trees could look! How mightily they can stand there, how luxuriantly they blossom, how deeply they rustle, how luscious and complete the shadows they cast, how they swell with monstrous fullness in the summer and lay down their golden-brown leaves in such thick, soft piles in the fall!

Today I am once again thinking of the city with the beautiful chestnut trees: a town in southwest Germany. In the center is the old castle, a massive sprawling boxy structure, with the whole sprawling building ringed by an amazingly wide moat, long since turned into a dry ditch, and surrounding the ditch in a wider circle is a splendid avenue. On one side of the avenue is nothing but old low houses and little gardens, and on the other, open side, facing the castle, is a mighty garland of large chestnut trees.

On one side hang signs for shops and inns, the joiners hammer away, metalworkers smash menacingly at their sheet metal, cobblers lurk in the twilight of their cavelike workshops, tanneries give off their mysterious stink. On the other side of the wide avenue there is silence and shade, the smell of leaves and the green play of light, the song of honeybees and the flight of butterflies. So the poor devils beating carpets and doing handicrafts have their windows facing an eternal holiday, the never-ending peace of God, and they squint longingly at it all the time, and on warm summer evenings they cannot go out to visit it early enough, or with enough sighs.

I stayed in that little city once, for a week, and although I was actually there on business, I liked to look patronizingly in through the merchants' and craftsmen's windows and put on a show of strolling—slowly, aristocratically, and often—on the shady, leisurely side of the street and of life. The best thing, though, was that I was staying by the moat, at the Blond Eagle, and had the many blossoming chestnut trees, red and white, outside my window in the evening and through the night. Now, enjoying this visual pleasure was not entirely without a cost, since the seemingly dry moat still had a damp enough moss-green bottom to send up a hundred thousand hungry mosquitoes a day. But a young person traveling doesn't sleep much on such summer nights anyway, and when the mosquitoes got too rude I rubbed some vinegar on myself and sat by the window with a cigar lit and the light off.

What singular evenings and nights! The smell of summer, a

little warm street dust, the buzz of mosquitoes, and mugginess filling the air with its electricity, secretly twitching and thrashing.

After all these years, those warm nights along the chestnut alley now come back to me and seem precious and poignant, like an island in my life, a fairy tale, a lost youth. They look at me with a gaze so deep and holy; their whisper is so beguilingly sweet and hot; they make me so sad, like the legend of paradise or the lost song that dreams of Avalon.

I would usually be finished with my "business" by the afternoon. As soon as that moment came, I would stroll the whole circle around the castle once or twice with the gentlemanly hauteur of the idle do-nothing, enjoying the freedom and laziness I felt such a talent for in those days. Oh, if I'm ever going to accomplish anything in life (but is that really as very necessary as everyone's always telling me?)—if I am, I will have to work so hard, so bitterly, that surely I can now enjoy the gift of these few free days . . .

Then I would saunter off through the city and the park outside town, and up some hill to a high fragrant summer meadow or dim, secret corner of the woods. The squirrels racing like lightning, the tumbling butterflies—I hadn't looked at them with so much idle abandonment since I was a boy. I would swim in a brook, or at least splash water on my warm head. Then, in some hidden spot, I would take out a little notebook of graph paper and write in it with my sharpest pencil things I was ashamed of, but which nonetheless made me unbelievably happy, even proud. Presumably my poetry from then was worthless, and I'd probably laugh if I saw any of it again today. . . . No, I wouldn't laugh. Definitely not. But I wish I could ever be as crazily silly, giddy, and deeply happy again when I was writing or, indeed, doing anything.

And so evening would come, and I'd walk back into town. I would pick a rose in the park and carry it in my hand, for how easily it might happen that I would find myself in a situation where one wants to have a rose in one's hand. For instance, if I ran into Kiderlen the carpenter's daughter on the market corner at a propitious moment, and I doffed my hat, and maybe she didn't just nod but let a conversation spring up, would I have any qualms about offering her that rose with some suitable words? Or maybe it might be Martha, the niece and waitress at the Eagle—it was because of her that they had renamed the Black Eagle Inn as the Blond. She always looked down on me so. But maybe she wasn't really like that.

Lost in such thoughts, I would enter the city and walk back and forth through the few little streets, inviting Chance to show its face, before returning to the Eagle. As I walked up to the door of the inn I would stick my rose in my buttonhole and then enter, and politely order ham with mustard or a ham hock or ribs with cabbage, and a Vaihinger beer to go with it.

I would page back through my little book of verses until the food came, quickly putting a line in the margin or a question mark or crossing something out here and there, and then I would eat and drink and take the older, more elegant gentlemen among the regulars as my model for proper conversation and conduct. It sometimes happened that the innkeeper, husband or wife, would do more than wish me bon appétit, they would sit down across from me for a bit and start a conversation. I would answer their questions, affable but modest, and I could occasionally manage to offer a pithy saying, a political opinion, a joke.

Finally I would pay for my dinner, take a bottle of lager with me, and go upstairs to my room. The mosquitoes would be whirring busily. I would have to stick my beer in the washbasin's water to keep it cool.

Then came those strange evening hours. I sat on the windowsill, alone, and half-consciously felt how beautiful the summer night was, and the slight mugginess, and the ghostly pale beacons of the chestnut's white blossoms, like large candles. Then, anxious and melancholy, I would see the couples walking in the dark under the great trees, slowly, pressed up against each other, and I would sadly take my rose from its buttonhole and throw it out the window, onto the slightly dusty, shimmering white road for carriages and guests from the inn and lovers to trample.

Have I promised to tell you a story here? No, I promised nothing of the sort, nor do I want to tell any stories. You can tell a story about getting engaged or breaking your leg. I want only to hear the song of those summer nights once more—it is dearer to me than all the songs of Avalon put together. I want only to call back to mind the old city, and the castle, and the moat, so I don't forget them forever. I want only to think about those chestnut trees for a little while, after all these years, and about my little poetry notebook, and all of that, because it will never return.

But it does seem unbelievable that I only spent seven days and nights there. It feels like I took at least a hundred walks up to the woods, broke off at least a hundred roses, planned to give at least a hundred roses on a hundred evenings to the pretty girls in the chestnut-tree city and then gloomily threw them out onto the darkening street later, when no one wanted them. Of course I'd stolen those roses, but who would have known that? Not Kiderlen the carpenter's daughter, not blond Martha, and if one of them had wanted that stolen rose from me, I would have gladly bought a hundred more to give her.

PLATE 9

# DREAM

Every time I have the same dream:
A redly blossoming chestnut tree,
A garden full of summer flowers,
An old house whiling lonely hours.

There, in the garden's quiet deep,
My mother used to rock me to sleep.
But maybe—it happened so long before—
Garden, house, tree are all no more.

Maybe now a path through a meadow
Runs over the place, or plow and harrow.
From home and garden, house and tree
Nothing is left except my dream.

PLATE 10

# THE PEACH TREE

ast night the foehn wind surged mighty and merciless
across the patient countryside, over empty fields and gardens, through barren grapevines and bare forests, tearing at
every bough and trunk, howling and snarling at every obstacle;
it rattled like a skeleton in the fig tree and whirled clouds of
withered leaves up into the sky. In the morning those leaves
lay tidily gathered into large piles, crouched low and pressed
flat, behind every corner, every protruding wall, anywhere that
offered shelter from the wind.

When I went out to the garden, I saw that disaster had struck.
My largest peach tree had come down, broken off close to the
ground, and now it lay aslant on the steep embankment of the
vineyard. Peach trees don't grow to be all that old, and they
do not rank among the giants and heroes—they are delicate
and vulnerable, oversensitive to injuries, and their resiny sap
has something of ancient, overrefined aristocratic blood about
it. The one lying there wasn't an especially noble or lovely tree,
but it had been, after all, my biggest peach tree, an old friend,
making its home on this plot of land for longer than I've been
here. Every year, soon after the middle of March, it had opened
its buds and shown its rosily blooming, frothy crown set off
against the sky—vibrantly against the fair-weather blue, with
infinite delicacy against the gray of a rainy day. It had shud-
dered in the sportive gusts of brisk April days, with the golden

yellow flames of brimstone butterflies passing through it; it had braced itself against the wicked foehn, stood quiet and dreamy in the wet gray of the rain, slightly stooped, looking down at its feet where the grass of the steep vineyard slope turned greener and fatter with every rainy day. Sometimes I'd taken a little blossoming branch inside and kept it in my room; sometimes I'd propped the tree up with a pole in the season when its fruits began to weigh too heavily on the branches; sometimes too, in earlier years, I'd been bold enough to try to paint it when it blossomed. All through the year it had stood there, occupying its place in my little world, where it too belonged; it had lived through heat and snow, storm and calm, had added its note to the song, its sound to the picture; it had gradually far outgrown the vineyard's low posts, outlasted generations of squirrels and snakes, birds and butterflies. It was not exceptional, not much noticed or particularly honored, but it had been indispensable. Around when the fruit was beginning to ripen, I would take the little detour from the tiny path ending at my steps over to that tree, bend down to the wet grass, pick up the peaches that had fallen in the night, and bring them back up to the house in my pocket, in a basket, or even in my hat, and set them out in the sun on the terrace railing.

Now, in the place that had once belonged to this old friend, there was a hole—the little world had a little rip in it, through which the void, the darkness, death and horror could peek in. The broken trunk lay there sadly, its wood looking crumbly and a little spongy; the branches had cracked and bent in the fall, branches which in maybe two weeks would have once again borne their rosy-red crown of spring and held it up against the blue or gray sky. Never again would I break off a branch from it, pluck a peach from it, never again try to draw the capricious and somewhat fantastical structure of its branching, never again walk over to it from my stairs on a hot summer afternoon to rest in its thin shade for a moment. I shouted for Lorenzo, the gardener, and told him to bring the fallen tree to the barn. There, on the next rainy day, when there was nothing else that needed doing, it would get sawed into firewood. In a bad mood, I watched him. There is nothing we can count on in this world, not even trees! They, too, can abandon you, die on you, leave you in the lurch one day and cross over into the great darkness and vanish forever!

I watched Lorenzo struggling to drag the trunk away. Farewell, my dear peach tree! At least you died an honest, natural, and proper death, and I'm happy to commend you for it—you withstood and endured until you could no longer and the great enemy twisted your limbs from their sockets. You had no choice but to give in. You fell and were severed from your roots. But you weren't shattered by bombs dropped from planes, incinerated by devilish acids, torn from the soil of your home like millions of others and fleetingly replanted, roots bleeding, only to be caught and made homeless again; you did not have to experience the apocalypse and destruction, war and desecration around you, and die in misery in the end. You had a fate suitable to your kind. I'm happy to commend you for it: you grew old better and more beautifully, and died with more dignity, than us. We have to defend ourselves in our old age against the poison and misery of a pestilential world, have to fight to wrest every breath of fresh clean air from the rot devouring all around us.

When I saw the tree lying on the ground, I thought, as I always did after such losses, about replacement, replanting. We would dig a hole where the fallen tree used to be, and leave it open to the sun and rain and air for a good long while; over time we would throw into the hole some dung, compost from the pile of weeds, different kinds of garbage mixed in with the ashes from the woodstove, and then one day, preferably in a soft, warm rain, we would plant a new young sapling. The air and the soil here would suit that sapling, that young tree, just as well, and it too would become a friend and good neighbor to the vineyard, the flowers, the squirrels and birds and butterflies, would bear fruit in a few years, would put out its dear blossoms every spring in the second half of March, and, if fate smiled upon it, would one day fall victim as an old, tired tree to some storm or landslide or weight of snow.

But this time I couldn't bring myself to replant here. I'd planted plenty of trees in my life; one more or less wouldn't matter. And something inside me resisted renewing the cycle again, here too, this time too, giving another push to the wheel of life and cultivating one more new prey for ravenous death. I didn't want to. Let the place stand empty.

## IN FULL FLOWER

The cherry tree is in full flower;
Not every blossom will turn to fruit.
Like a foam of roses they shimmer bright
Through the blue sky and the drifting clouds.

Our thoughts arise like cherry blossoms,
Hundreds every single day—
Let them bloom! Let each run its course
And do not ask what it might bring!

This game must be played in innocence,
Must flower in pure exuberance,
Or else the world would be much too small,
And this life of ours no joy at all.

PLATE 11

# HERMITS AND WARRIORS

I saw meadows and slopes and earth-brown ravines covered with grasses, flowers, ferns, and mosses, to which the old local dialect had given strange and portentous names. These plants, the children and grandchildren of the mountains, lived in their proper places, colorful and harmless, and I touched them, observed them, smelled their scents, and learned their names. I was more deeply moved by the sight of the trees, though. I saw every one of them leading a life of its own, taking on its own particular shape and crown, casting its own individual shadow. I felt they were more closely related to the mountains, as hermits and warriors themselves, for every tree, especially the ones higher up the mountains, had its own silent stubborn war to wage against wind and weather and rock if it was to survive and grow. Each had its burden to bear and had to cling tight to the slopes, giving each its own shape and particular wounds. There were Scotch pines that storms had let put forth their branches only on one side, and others whose red trunks curved around overhanging rocks like snakes so that tree and rock held each other tight in an embrace that saved them both. These trees looked upon me as though they were warlike men, awakening awe and respect in my heart.

Our men and women were like these trees: hard, severely wrinkled, and saying little—the best of them saying the least. From this I learned to look upon people as trees, or cliffs: to contemplate them, and honor them no less, love them no more, than I did the quiet pines.

# SHACKLED POWER AND PASSION

M y path led onward to the edge of the forest, the windward side, and I amused myself looking at the bold, meaningfully grotesque forms of the trunks, boughs, and roots. Nothing can occupy the imagination more strongly or deeply. At first, humorous impressions predominate: hideous grimaces and recognizable caricatures of well-known faces in the convolutions of the roots, the crevices in the soil, the pictures formed by branches, the masses of foliage. Then the eye grows sharper and sees, without trying, whole hosts of strange forms. The comic element disappears, for all these images look so resolute, so bold and implacable, that the silent throng soon proclaims itself to be following greater laws and grave necessity. Finally, the shapes turn eerily accusatory and uncanny. It is always the same: the changeable human being who wears so many masks flinches in horror as soon as he or she looks, closely and seriously, at the traits of any naturally grown thing.

# THE BIRCH

A poet's tangled weave of dreams
Couldn't spread into finer branches,
Couldn't bend more easily in the wind,
Couldn't rise more nobly to the sky.

Delicate, young, and so very slim,
Subdued and timid and shy:
You let these long light branches hang
For every breeze to set atremble.

Rocking gently, softly swaying,
You offer me with your delicate tremor
An image, beautiful and pure,
Of the love I felt when I was young.

PLATE 12

# MAY IN THE CHESTNUT FOREST

Now, in early May, and again in late autumn, the southern mountain landscape has its most beautiful days. Throughout the summer, all the hills and smaller mountains are wooded. The whole countryside is green then, green green green, and if it weren't for the colorful villages shining forth everywhere in its midst, and a couple of snow-covered peaks peeking over from a distance, it would be almost boring. Now, on the other hand, with the chestnut trees just beginning to get their leaves, with the forest as a whole still slightly transparent, with the last wild cherry trees in blossom and the first acacias starting to bloom—now the southern forest is charming, its burningly fresh green spilling over into the red, still so thin and provisional, still letting the sky and the stars and the distant mountains show through everywhere.

The king of the forest, during this time, is the cuckoo. Everywhere in the quiet lonely valleys, on the sunny wooded peaks, in the shady ravines you can hear his deep voice paying court. His call means it is spring, his song sings immortality, it is not for nothing that we ask him the number of years we will live. His voice rings through the woods, warm and deep, and here in the Southern Alps it sounds no different than it did during my childhood in the Black Forest and the Rhine Valley, or than it did during my years on Lake Constance, where my sons heard it for the first time when they were children. It has remained the same, like the sun, like the forest, like the green of fresh leaves and the violet and white of drifting May clouds. Year after year the cuckoo calls, and nobody knows if it's the same one as last year, or what has become of the cuckoos we once heard as children, as schoolboys, as young men.

Back then this propitious deep voice sounded of promise and future, of courtship, of coming storms, of approaching happiness; now it sounds like the past. It is all the same to the bird whether he cries his exhortations to us or our children or grandchildren—whether his scream wakes us in our cradles or sings over our graves. He is rarely to be seen, this shy brother, and for that alone I love him. He doesn't show himself easily; he wants to stay by himself. For practically everyone, the cuckoo is nothing but this beautiful, deep, seductive voice in the green—they have heard him thousands and thousands of times but never seen him. Yesterday I asked a whole pack of twelve-year-old schoolboys if they'd ever seen a cuckoo, and only a single one said yes.

But I've seen him many times, this shy brother, my cheerful forest cousin who remains invisible to most and about whom are told such charmingly fresh and widespread stories. Though invisible, he still reigns as king of the whole forest for two months. A ringing, defiant herald of love, he cares little for marriage, home, and child-rearing. Keep calling, Brother Cuckoo, you are one of my favorite animals. I'm on good terms with all kinds of animals, it must be said, even though I myself am a predator—I get along with them all, know many of them well, have games I play with many, including the shy and lesser-known kinds—even the fearful and yet so brazen little high-land fox doesn't escape my notice.* This year I have managed to see the cuckoo again, and not just one but a pair, him and her. I saw them from the bottom of a gully where I was picking may-flowers; I stood as still as a dried-up tree for a long while, and they didn't notice me. They were playing, chasing each other up and down through the high treetops (there are tall ash trees, too, here and there amid the chestnut forest). Their cheerful, sinuous flights looped in celebratory garlands—the large dark birds, stretched out straight, raced from tree to tree in wild and always surprising twists and turns, suddenly plunging vertically to the ground, suddenly rocketing straight up to the treetops, and every few moments they would stop and perch, for less than a second, and blurt out their sharp, excited cry.

I didn't catch sight of the cuckoo every year of my life—all in all it must have been a dozen times—and we won't meet up very often again: my legs don't work as well as they used to, and before long shy Brother Cuckoo will have only my sons and grandchildren to sing to. Listen well, grandchildren: He knows a lot, learn from him! Learn from him the bold spring flight that quivers with joy, the warm wooing cry of seduction, the far-ranging life of the wanderer, the contempt for philistines, including the little fox from the highland!

---

* This "highland fox" (*Hochlandfuchs*), mentioned again at the end of the next paragraph, is actually an allusion to Friedrich Fuchs, the editor of a magazine called *Hochland*, who had attacked Hesse in print. —Translator.

Every day I spend a few hours in the forest. Already, the Solomon's seal and mayflowers and spotted orchids are blooming alongside the anemones and lungwort. Sometimes I paint in the forest, sometimes I lie in the grass and sleep, sometimes I lie and read.[...]

Soon it will be summer here. Soon the forest will have grown together into a dense, lush green, and the thin, delicate forest grass will have sprung up high in the clearings, and at night I will hear the owl call. . . . The owl is another bird I have great respect for, no less than the cuckoo. It, too, is shy, rarely visible, and it knows the secret of flying in silence as smooth and dreamlike as a cloud's, and besides it is a bird of prey, with sharp, strong talons and beak, and more intelligent than many other animals, not to speak of human beings. Soon it will be summer, new notes will fill the forest, new scents, new colors, and what today surges out of the ground green and small and germinating will then be old and stiff and brown. The cuckoo, too, will fall silent—it too—and only the sun will still shine, and the stars, and publishers will still, just like before, send out copies of their excellent books.

PLATE 13

# THE BLACK FOREST

Strangely lovely flights of hills,
Darker mountains, brighter meadows,
Reddish cliffs and brown ravines,
Brushed with shadows from firs!

When overhead a soaring spire
Blends the sound of its pious bells
With the stormy rustling of a fir tree
I can stop and listen long.

Then, the way an ancient saga
Read at night by the fire does,
My memory seizes on the days
When once I made this place my home.

When distances were nobler, softer,
When mountains wreathed in a forest of fir
Were holier and richer, too,
Glittering in my child eyes.

# Trees

I think that I shall never see
A poem lovely as a tree.

A tree whose hungry mouth is prest
Against the earths sweet flowing breast;

A tree that looks at God all day,
And lifts her leafy arms to pray;

A tree that may in Summer wear
A nest of robins in her hair;

Upon whose bosom snow has lain,
Who intimately lives with rain.

Poems are made by fools like me,
But only God can make a tree.

· Joyce Kilmer

( Der amerikanische Dichter
Dieser Verse fiel im
ersten Weltkrieg )

*Hesse's handwritten copy of the poem by Joyce Kilmer (1886–1918),
an American poet who died in France during WW I at age 31.* —Editor.

## "TREES" BY JOYCE KILMER

I think that I shall never see
A poem lovely as a tree.

A tree whose hungry mouth is prest
Against the earth's sweet flowing breast;

A tree that looks at God all day,
And lifts her leafy arms to pray;

A tree that may in Summer wear
A nest of robins in her hair;

Upon whose bosom snow has lain,
Who intimately lives with rain.

Poems are made by fools like me,
But only God can make a tree.

# UPROOTED

Over there an old inn stood alone. I recognized its roof from afar, looking the same as it always had yet strangely different somehow, and at first I didn't know why. Only when I thought it over more carefully did I remember that there had always been two tall poplars in front of the inn. These poplars were no longer there. An age-old view I had always known had been destroyed, a place I loved desecrated.

And I felt an evil premonition: that more things, even nobler, might have also been ruined. Suddenly, oppressively, I could again feel how much I loved my old home, how deeply my heart and well-being depended on these roofs and towers, bridges and lanes, trees and parks and forests. Newly worried and agitated, I ran fast until I reached the fairground.

There I stopped and saw the site of my most treasured memories completely destroyed—an anonymous, ravaged wasteland. The old chestnut trees in whose shade we'd had our festivals, whose trunks even three or four of us schoolboys couldn't hold hands in a ring around, lay there broken off, shattered, their roots torn out and upturned, leaving gaping holes in the

*previous* PLATE 14

ground the size of houses. Not one still stood —it was a gruesome battlefield—and the lindens and maples had fallen too, tree after tree. The large square was a monstrous rubble heap of branches, split trunks, roots, and blocks of earth; mighty trunks still stood upright but with their crowns snapped or twisted off, sporting only a thousand bare white splinters.

It was impossible to walk any farther. The square and the streets were blocked with trunks and pieces of trees thrown helter-skelter in piles as high as buildings, and where since my earliest childhood I had known only deep, sacred shade and tall tree temples, now the empty sky stared down upon the annihilation.

It felt like I, too, had been torn out, with all my secret roots spat into the merciless glare of day. I walked around all day and found no forest path anymore, no beloved walnut-tree shade, none of the oaks we used to climb as boys—everywhere around the city for a great distance there was rubble, holes, broken forest slopes mowed down like grass, the corpses of trees with their uncovered rootwork pitifully turned toward the sun. A chasm had opened up between me and my childhood, and my homeland was no longer the old one. The charm and folly of those years of the past fell away from me, and not long afterward I left that city, to become a man and to face life, whose first shadows had brushed me during those days.

## PAGE FROM A DIARY

Today on the hill behind the house
I cut and dug a ditch through roots
And Steinicht stone, made it deep enough,
And took out every rock, and then
Removed the thin and crumbly dirt.
Then I kneeled awhile, now here, now there
In the old woods, gathering with scoop
And hands from moldering chestnut trunks
That black decaying forest soil
With its smell of mushrooms warm and rich,
Two heavy buckets full, and carried it
Back, and planted a tree in the ditch,
Packed the peaty soil tenderly around it,
Slowly poured on it some sun-warmed water,
And gently soaked and dredged the roots in.

There it stands, still young; there it will stand
When we are gone, when our busy days
Of noisy splendor and endless adversity
And all their crazy terrors are long forgotten.
The foehn wind will bend it, storm winds tousle it,
Sun laugh upon it, wet snow weigh it down,
The finch and nuthatch, too, will live there,
The quiet hedgehog burrow at its feet.

And all that it lives through, savors, and endures
In the course of the years—changing generations
Of animals, oppression and relief,

The friendship of the wind and of the sun—
Will pour out from it, every day, in the song
Of its rustling leaves, in the friendly gesture
Of its gently waving treetop,
In the sweet scent of the resinous sap
That wets the buds stuck shut with sleep,
In the endless game of light and shadow
It happily plays against itself.

## LINDEN BLOSSOMS

Now the lindens truly are in bloom again, and in the evening, when it starts to get dark and when the day's hard work is done, the women and children come over, climb ladders up to the branches, and pluck a little basket full of linden blossoms. Later, when someone is sick and needs it, they will make from these blossoms a healthy curative tea. They are right—why should the warmth, the sun, the joy, and the fragrance of this wondrous season pass away without anyone making good use of it? Why shouldn't some of it tangibly remain, condensed in blossoms or somewhere else, that we can gather and bring home and later, in cold and evil times, get some consolation from?

If only we could store up a bagful of every beautiful thing and save it until we had need of it! Of course they would merely be artificial flowers with artificial scent. Every day the fullness of the world rushes past us; every day flowers bloom, light beams, joy laughs. Sometimes we drink our fill of it, sometimes we're tired and sullen and don't want

**PLATE 15**

to hear anything about it; always, though, an excess of beauty surrounds us. That is the splendid thing about all our joys: they come unearned and undeserved, they cannot be bought or corrupted, they are free, a gift of God to everyone, like the fragrance of linden blossoms in the breeze.

The women industriously crouching in the branches gathering the blossoms end up with a tea that helps against shortness of breath and fever, but the best and finest part they do not have. Not even the couples in love, taking pleasure strolls on summer evenings in their dull sweet drunkenness, have it. But the wanderer who passes by and takes a deeper breath— he does. The wanderer has the best and most subtle part of all pleasures, for along with the enjoyment he has the knowledge of how fleeting all joy is. It doesn't bother him much that he cannot drink at every spring; he is accustomed to excess, so he doesn't keep gazing at what was lost; he doesn't immediately want to put down roots everywhere there's something good. That kind of traveler exists, taking pleasure trips year after year to the same place, and there are many people who can't say good-bye to a beautiful view without vowing to come back again soon. They might be perfectly good people, but they are not good wanderers. They have something of the dull drunkenness of the lovers and something of the painstaking collector's spirit of the women picking the linden blossoms. But they do not have the wanderer's soul—quiet, earnestly cheerful, always saying good-bye.

Someone wandered through here yesterday, an itinerant journeyman, who in his beggar's freedom mockingly greeted the blossom-gatherers and other locals. At the big linden tree full of women on the branches he took the ladder away and walked off, and even though I was the one who had to carry the ladder back for the women and placate them as they cursed and railed, the joke amused me anyway.

Oh, you itinerant journeymen, you merry light-footed spirits, I watch every last one of you, even if I've just given you a fiver, walk away as if you were a king— with respect, admiration, and envy. Every one of you, even the most ragged and rundown, wears an invisible crown; every one of you is a happy man and a conqueror. I too was once like you, and I know what wandering feels like, what strange new places feel like. They taste sweet indeed, despite all the homesickness and deprivation and uncertainty.

And all the while, the honey-sweet scent pours out of the old trees along the roadside through the warm summer evening. Children are singing down by the shore and playing with red and yellow paper pinwheels. Couples walk slowly and nonchalantly along the hedgerows. Honeybees and bumblebees whir in ecstatic circles through the red-gold dust of the street, humming their golden notes.

But the truth is, I do not envy the couples by the hedgerows their sweet dull drunkenness, nor the children their unaccountable bliss, nor the swarming bees their tumbling flight. The only ones I envy are the itinerant journeymen. They have the fragrance, the florescence, of all the rest.

To be young, inexperienced, unattached, reckless, and curious again, to go running out into the world, to scarf down meals of cherries on the side of the road and decide where to go at the crossroads by counting off "Left, right, left, right" on the buttons of your shirt! To spend short warm fragrant summer nights on the road sleeping in haystacks again, to spend time wandering in harmless concord with the birds of the forest, the squirrels, and the beetles! Now, that would be worth a summer and a pair of new boot soles. But it cannot be. There is no use in singing the old songs, swinging the old walking stick, walking the dear old dusty streets, and imagining you're young again and everything is the way it was.

No, that's gone. Not that I've gotten old, or turned into a philistine! If anything, I am probably more foolish, self-indulgent, and unrestrained than ever, and there is no more mutual understanding or connection than before between me and the clever people with all their business. So too I still hear the voice of life calling and exhorting me as much as it did in the most urgent time of my young manhood, and I have no intention of being untrue to that voice. But it no longer calls me to wander, to friendship, to bacchanals with song and torchlight; now it is soft and urgent and leads me along ever more solitary, darker, quieter paths, and I still don't know if those paths will end in pleasure or sorrow, only that I want to walk them, and walk them I must.

I had pictured adulthood so differently when I was young. Now it, too, turns out to be a time of waiting, questioning, restlessness, more longing than fulfillment. The linden blossoms give off their scent, and itinerant journeymen, flower-gatherers, children, and lovers all seem to obey their law and know what they're about. I'm the only one who doesn't know what he's supposed to do. I know only that neither the unaccountable bliss of the playing children nor the indifferent passing of the wanderer, neither the dull drunkenness of the lovers nor the painstaking collector's spirit of the women plucking flowers is my allotted fate. Mine is to follow the voice of life calling within me—even if I cannot tell its direction or its goal, and even if it leads me ever farther from the merry street off into uncertainty and darkness.

# LAMENT FOR AN OLD TREE

For almost ten years now, since the end of our jaunty recent war, my daily society, my constant familiar interactions have no longer been with other people. I don't lack for friends, men and women, it's true, but my contact with them is a special occasion, not an everyday occurrence. They visit me every now and then, or I visit them, but I've broken the habit of continual living with other people. I live alone, and so in my little daily dealings, things have more and more come to take the place of people. The walking stick with which I ramble, the cup from which I drink my milk, the vase on my table, the bowl of fruit, the ashtray, the floor lamp with its green shade, the little Indian bronze Krishna, the pictures on the wall, and, to save the best for last, the many books on the shelves in my little home—these are what keep me company when I wake up and when I go to sleep, as I eat or work, on good days and bad; these are the familiar faces I see, these are what give me the pleasant illusion of having my place in the world, of being at home.

Many, many other objects are my close companions, too: things I like to see and feel, whose mute service and mute language are dear to me and seem indispensable. When one of these things abandons me and leaves—when an old bowl

PLATE 16

breaks, a vase falls, a pocketknife gets lost—it is a real loss for me. I have to say my good-bye and reflect for a moment and give the thing a fitting eulogy.

My writing room, too, with its somewhat slanting walls, its old, totally faded golden wallpaper, the many cracks in its plaster ceiling—it, too, is one of my companions and friends. It is a beautiful room, and I would be lost if it were taken from me. But the most beautiful thing about it is the opening leading out to the little balcony. From there I can see not only Lake Lugano all the way to San Mamette, with all the bays and mountains and villages, dozens of villages near and far, but also—and this is what is dearest to me—I can look down into an old, quiet, enchanted garden where venerable old trees rock in the wind and the rain, where lovely tall palm trees, lush and lovely camellias, rhododendrons, and magnolias grow on narrow terraces on a steep hill, where the yew, the copper beech, the Indian willow, the tall evergreen Korean mountain magnolia grow. Even more than my room and my objects, this view, these terraces and bushes and trees, belong to me and my life, are my actual circle of friends, my closest companions—I live with them, they stick by me, I can count on them. And when I look out over this garden, the sight gives me more than it gives to the charmed or indifferent gaze of a stranger, infinitely more, for I know this picture intimately, I have seen it year after year, at every hour of the day and night, in every season, every weather. The leaves of every tree as well as their flowers and fruit, in every state of their growth and dying off, I know them all well; every one is a friend, there are secrets about every last one that I and I alone know. Losing one of these trees is to me like losing a friend.[...]

There is a time in the spring when the garden is flaming red with camellia flowers, and in the summer the palms bloom and blue wisteria climb high up all the trees. But the Indian willow, a small exotic tree that despite its modest size looks ancient, seems to be freezing for half the year and doesn't venture to put out its leaves until late; it doesn't begin to bloom before somewhere around mid-August.

Yet the most beautiful tree of all is not there anymore—a few days ago it broke in a storm. A heavy old giant with a cracked and tattered trunk, it hasn't been cleared away; I can see it lying there and see where it used to stand a wide gap, through which come glimpses of the distant chestnut forest and a few previously invisible huts.

It was a Judas tree, the kind the Savior's betrayer hanged himself on, but you couldn't see these anguished origins by looking—no, it was the most beautiful tree in the garden, and actually it was for that tree's sake that I rented this apartment some years ago. At the time, with the war just ended, I came to this region alone, as a refugee; my old life had fallen apart, and I was looking for a place to stay where I could work and think back and rebuild the shattered world for myself from within. I was looking for a little apartment, and when I saw where I live now it was nice enough, but the decisive moment came when the landlady led me out onto the little balcony. There beneath me was suddenly Klingsor's garden, and right in the middle of it glowed a giant flowering tree, light pink, whose name I immediately asked the landlady for, and lo and behold it was the Judas tree, and year after year since then it bloomed, millions of rosy-pink flowers sitting close to the bark, a little like daphnes, and the flowers lasted four to six weeks, and only then came the light-green leaves, and later dense throngs of mysterious dark-purple pods would hang amid these leaves.

If you look up "Judas tree" in the dictionary, you naturally don't find much that's intelligent or sensible. Not a word about Judas and the Savior! Instead it says that this tree belongs to the legume family and is known as Cercis siliquastrum, that its habitat is southern Europe, and that here and there it is used as an ornamental shrub. Oh, and also that another name for it is "false carob" or "false St. John's bread." God only knows how the genuine Judas and the false St. John got mixed up! But when I read the words "ornamental shrub" I have to laugh, even in the midst of my lamentations. Ornamental shrub! It was a tree, a giant of a tree, with a trunk thicker than I've ever seen at the best of times, and its treetop rose up from the garden's deep ravine almost to the height of my little balcony. It was a magnificent specimen, a real mast! I wouldn't have wanted to be standing under that "ornamental shrub" when it broke in the recent storm and came crashing down like an old lighthouse.[. . .]

One night, as the late aftermath of some American hurricane from across the ocean, a wild southern storm came blowing up—it ripped apart the vineyards, toppled chimneys, even demolished my little stone balcony, and then, at the last moment, took down my old Judas tree as well. I still remember how as a boy I loved it so much when these preternaturally terrifying equinoctial storms used to blow in the wonderful Romantic stories by Hauff or E.T.A. Hoffmann! Alas, that was just how it was in real life: it was that heavy, that preternatural, and the thick wind as hot as if from the desert bore down wild and claustrophobic on our peaceful valley, causing its American mischief. It was an ugly night, no one in the whole village except the babies got a minute of sleep, and in the morning broken bricks and shattered windowpanes and snapped-off grapevines lay everywhere. But the worst, most irreparable thing for me was the destruction of the Judas tree. A younger brother will be replanted there, yes, that has already been arranged, but before it is half as stately as its predecessor, I will be long gone.

PLATE 17

PLATE 18

PLATE 19

PLATE 20

# VAGRANT HOSTEL

How strange and wonderful it is
That never ceasing, every night,
The quiet fountain keeps flowing forth
Guarded by the cool shade of the maple tree.

And again and again, like scent, the moonlight
Rests upon the house's gables,
And through the chilly, dark air flies
The wispy flock of passing clouds!

That everything is, that everything lasts,
While we, we merely stay for a night
And then walk on, across the land,
None paying us another thought.

And then, perhaps after many a year,
A fountain comes to us in a dream,
And gate, and gable, the way it was
And still is and for long shall be.

It shines out at us like a sense of home,
And yet it was just a short night's rest,
A stranger's roof for a passing stranger
Who's forgotten the inn's name, even its city.

How strange and wonderful it is
That never ceasing, every night,
The quiet fountain keeps flowing forth
Guarded by the cool shade of the maple tree!

PLATE 21

# OPPOSITES

I t is high summer, and for weeks already the big Korean mountain magnolia outside my window has been in bloom. With its seemingly slow, apparently relaxed and indifferent, but actually quick and extravagantly wasteful manner of blooming, it is a perfect symbol of the southern summer. The gigantic snow-white clusters of flowers always have only a few blossoms open at a time, at most eight or ten, so the tree looks the same during the whole two months of its blooming season despite the splendid, giant flowers being actually so ephemeral: none lives longer than two days. It usually opens from its pale, greenish-tinged bud in the early morning; pure white, enchantingly unreal, it floats out from the hard, dark, shining, evergreen leaves, reflecting the light like the snowy Atlas, young and aglow for a day and then gently starting to lose its shape and change color, yellowing around the edges. It ages expressing a resignation and exhaustion that is quite moving, and this period of growing old likewise lasts only a day. Then the white flower is already discolored, a light cinnamon brown, and the petals, yesterday like Atlas, now feel like fine suede: a marvelous dreamlike material, delicate as a breath and yet a firm, solid, even coarse substance. And so my big magnolia tree bears its pure snowy flowers day after day, and they always seem to be the same ones. A fine, thrilling, exquisite scent, like that of fresh lemons but sweeter, wafts over from these flowers into my writing room.

But the big Korean mountain magnolia (a summer magnolia not to be confused with the spring magnolias that also grow in the north) is not always my friend, however beautiful it might be. There are times of year when I look at it with misgivings, even hostility. It grows and grows, and in the ten years it's been my neighbor it has extended so far that my balcony has lost what little morning sun it used to have in the autumn and spring months. It has turned into a giant hulk of a fellow; in its heavy, lush growth it often reminds me of a rough, gangly boy who's shot up in height. Now, though, during its high-summer blooming season, it stands there in full, delicate, ceremonious dignity, clattering its stiff, shining, lacquered-looking leaves in the wind, and taking special care to tend gingerly to its delicate, all-too-beautiful, all-too-ephemeral flowers.

Confronting this big tree, with its gigantic pale flowers, is another tree, a dwarf. This one is on my little balcony, planted in a pot: a squat dwarf tree, a variety of cypress, less than three feet tall despite being almost forty years old—little, gnarled, self-assured, somewhat touching and somewhat comic, full of dignity and yet crotchety and a little ridiculous. I was recently given it as a gift, for my birthday, and there it stands, sticking out its gnarled branches full of character and seemingly bent by decades-long storms yet no longer than a finger; it calmly gazes out across the garden at its giant brother, two of whose flowers would be enough to cover the worthy dwarf completely. But it doesn't mind that, it doesn't seem to see big stout Brother

Magnolia at all, just one of whose leaves is as big as one of its own whole branches. The dwarf tree stands there in its strange little monumentality, deeply contemplative, entirely engrossed in itself, looking ancient, primeval, the same way people with dwarfism can sometimes look so unspeakably old or outside of time altogether.

In the terrible summer heat that's been besieging us for weeks I don't go out much; I live in my couple of rooms, behind closed shutters, and the two trees, giant and dwarf, are my company. The giant magnolia seems to me the emblem and siren song of all growth, all instinctive libidinal natural life, all carefree lusty fecundity. The taciturn dwarf facing it is its polar opposite, no doubt about it: it doesn't take up so much space, it squanders nothing, it strives for intensity and endurance; it is mind and spirit, not nature—conscious will, not instinctive drive. Dear little dwarf tree, how fantastical and judicious, tenacious and ancient you are!

Health, hard work, oblivious optimism that laughingly rejects all serious problems, a stout and cowardly refusal to aggressively pose questions, the art of living in the present—this is the watchword of our time, this is how our age tries to outwit the burdensome memory of the world war. Exaggeratedly easygoing, copying the Americans—an actor masked as a fat little baby—preeningly stupid, unbelievably happy and smiling: that is how this fashionable optimism stands there, adorned every day with radiant new flowers, the photos of new movie stars, the breaking of new records. That all these great things are merely of the moment, that all these pictures and records last only a day—no one cares, there'll be new ones tomorrow. And all this excessively stupid optimism, whipped up into its excessive frenzy, uninterested in any problems or anxieties, explaining away war and misery and death and pain as hooey and humbug that people only imagine—all this optimism, larger than life-size, cultivated and nurtured on the American model, stimulates and forces the spirit, in turn, into equally exaggerated states: redoubled critiques, deeper brooding on problems, a more hostile rejection of the whole rose-colored childlike worldview presented by the fashionable philosophers and illustrated tabloids.

So there I sit, between my tree neighbors, the wondrous vital magnolia and the wonderfully dematerialized, spiritualized dwarf, and I observe the play of opposites. I contemplate it, doze off a little in the heat, have a little smoke, and wait till it's evening and a little cool air blows in from the forest. And everywhere in what I do, read, think—everywhere I run into this same dichotomy of today's world. Every day letters come to me, from strangers mostly, well-meaning, sometimes accusatory, and all of them deal with the same problem: all are either from grotesque optimists, and they can't criticize or mock or feel sorry for me enough, hopeless pessimist that I am, or else they say I'm right, they fantastically and exaggeratedly agree with me, from the depths of their need and despair.[. . .]

They are both right, of course, both magnolia and dwarf tree, both optimists and pessimists. Only I think the former are more dangerous, because I can't look at their hearty self-satisfaction and full-bellied laughter without remembering that year of 1914 and the optimism, allegedly so healthy, with which whole nations back then found everything splendid and charming, and threatened to line all the pessimists up against the wall—the people who remembered, and reminded others, that wars are actually rather dangerous and violent undertakings and that things might end badly. Well, those pessimists were partly laughed at, partly lined up against the wall, and the optimists celebrated the great age they lived in, cheered and sang for years, until they had cheered themselves and their whole nations into exhaustion, and won to the point of exhaustion, and suddenly collapsed, and then they had to be consoled and encouraged to carry on by those same former pessimists. I can't ever quite forget that experience.

Of course we intellectuals and pessimists aren't right when all we do is reprimand and denounce our times, when we only condemn and sneer. But in the end, aren't we spiritual people (today they call us Romantics, and they don't mean anything positive by the term) a part of our times, with just as much right to speak for the age and embody a side of it as the championship boxers and car manufacturers? I am presumptuous enough to answer Yes.

These two trees, in their wonderful opposition, care nothing for oppositions. No natural things do. Each is sure of itself and its own rights; each is strong and stubborn. The magnolia swells with sap, and its flowers' sultry fragrance wafts over here. The dwarf tree withdraws still deeper into itself.

PLATE 22

# NIGHT WITH MOUNTAIN WIND

The fig tree rocks in the gusting foehn
Again like snakes the twisted boughs tangled;
The full moon rises over the barren cliff
To its lonely feast, quickens space with shadows,
Its light between drifting cloud-ships speaking
Dreamily to itself, enchanting the night
Above the Seetal to a quiet picture
Of soul and poetry, and deep within
My heart a music reawakens,
My soul rises up in urgent yearning,
Feels young, lusts to be back in surging life,
Struggles against fate, senses what it lacks,
Hums songs to itself, toys with dreams of bliss,
Wants to start over, wants to summon again
Distant youth's heat into the cooler present,
Wants to roam and woo and reach the stars
With the dark peal of its wide-ranging wishes.
I hesitate, then shut the window,
Put out the light, see the pale glow of pillow,
Know the moon above world and wafting cloud-poem
Outside, alive in the foehn above the silvery garden;
I slowly find my way back to normal life
And hear the song of my youth in my ears, until sleep.

# THE LITTLE PATH

A little path runs from the village down to the lake—a little footpath and goat path. I walk it often, hundreds of times all summer long and sometimes in winter, too.

The path is not that easy to find. It curves off from the road at a place where you wouldn't expect it, and the entrance to it, during the green season of the year, is entirely overgrown with a thicket of briars, bracken, and the ornamentation of mulberry branches. You push through this wilderness and the path drops quickly, quickly, almost vertically, through a sparse yet thick forest: a copse of young chestnut trees, all slender poles. Actually, they aren't young trees but ancient ones, only they were clear-cut decades ago and what now makes up this forest, and makes it look so funny and oddly bristly, are the thousands and thousands of young shoots rushing to spring out of the mighty old tree stumps. They are marvelous in May and early June, with their first young foliage; they have huge leaves, and the same way every one of those young chestnut shoots sticks up toward the sky in the exact same direction, as if combed, so the leaves fletching these arrows on both sides all point in one direction, and the whole sparse woods becomes a net of a hundred thousand lines all intersecting at the same angle.

*previous* PLATE 23

After a few minutes, you are already one terrace farther down the mountain, and here, on the edge of the woods, stand another couple of old chestnut trees—big, fatherly, noble trees with moss at their feet and ivy around their trunks and mighty crowns overhead—and lying at their feet, swept into piles, are the remains of last year's fruits: the prickly cups of last autumn's chestnuts. Next to them grows thin, very short, dry grass, a little steeply sloping meadow with its upper part in the shadow of the chestnut trees, its lower part in the sun. On this dry and often dusty little meadow there is always something pretty to see at the very start of spring: hundreds of thousands of very short, very fine, little white crocuses, a horde running down the rounded ridge of grass like silver fur, like a delicate breeze or a wisp of white mildew.

Past that meadow it is forest again. First, a copse of thin chestnuts, then acacias that in May smell like a tropical dream garden, with lots of holly mixed in, whose brassy leaves are so fat and shine so soothingly and whose red berries will glow through the bare woods during winter. The path turns very steep once more, and when it rains a wild brook runs along it down to the valley; that is why the little path is so deeply sluiced-out here. You walk as though in a deep gutter, a trench, with the rootstock of the chestnuts before your eyes, and alongside that you will find here and there in the autumn a lovely cèpe, its color the same as the withered leaves. But you need to go early and look well, because the people from the village go industriously hunting these mushrooms too, and toward the end of the summer on favorable days during the waxing moon they often go out as whole families and they have an admirable talent and skill for finding them, even though they can be so well hidden.

In June, this part of the woods is full of blueberries, and in a wide clearing where everything's been cut down it smells furtively like blueberries and heather all year long in sunny weather. Here too, in late summer, are the many colorful butterflies: scarlet tiger moth, painted lady.

Now the path gets less steep, running almost level for a while, and at the same time the forest itself gets tall and full. Beautiful old trees, including some ash trees, stand close together, spared; something remains of the brook here into the summer, along with a little pool, and a few flowers grow there that you can't find elsewhere in our mountains. The narrow little path rests and recuperates; it grows wider, in some places doubled, with a little twin, or *fratello*, running alongside it. Unexpectedly the old forest opens up: under its last trees there is a hut, a barn or shed, warm yellowish brown with a red roof, and when you step out from its shadow you find yourself on a little green terrace with short rows of grapevines separated by young peach trees and old mulberry trees cut back a hundred times, with venerable knots. You almost always see an old man here, standing on a short ladder wide at the base and pointed at the top, snipping away at these trees. His whole life long this old man has worked to prune them back so that the mulberry leaves would stay nice and close to the ground, easy to pick. And through all those years and decades the trees, snapped off and pruned, have put forth new shoots and grown anew and in the end they've won, they have grown taller after all, and the old man with his shears and saw will die without having truly vanquished them.

As you come out of the forest and walk across this little green terrace, past the vines and peaches and back toward the forest, there comes a beautiful moment when something red and blue and white shimmers through the lower woods, more or less depending on the season and leaf coverage. You then see, and gradually recognize, fiery red roofs far down below on the steep slope, a little village, and you hear the roosters crowing, and behind the village is a rosy beach, and the blue lake edged in white with a dull belt of reeds between the two, waving in the breeze. I always stop here a moment and stand and look, holding tight to a tree trunk, staring down, almost vertically, along the little, steeply descending path, across the red village roofs, the washing hung out to dry, and a reddish bocce court, out to the lake and the reeds.

After that it's just a few short hops, again through a narrow gutter and hollows thick with roots growing through them, under scattered old trees, to reach the open. Mulberry bushes conceal an old wall; climb over that and you've reached the blinding white road, and on the other side is the lake; the reeds sway, the boats float, and boys with bamboo fishing poles stand on tan legs in the shallow water.

# SUMMER AFTERNOON AT AN
# OLD COUNTRY HOUSE

Hundred-year-old lindens and chestnuts
Breathe and rustle softly in lukewarm wind,
The fountain flashes and turns complaisantly
In the breeze; up in the treetops
Are all the birds, almost silent for the moment.
The avenue outside, mute in midday heat;
The dogs outstretched and drowsy on the grass;
Distant hay carts creak across the land.

We sit in the shade a long time, we old people,
A book on our lap, our blinded eyes lowered,
Cradled sweetly by the summer day
But secretly thinking of things come before:
Neither winter nor summer day dawns for them now
But in the spacious rooms, along the paths,
They're still near us, invisible but present,
A bridge between Over There and Here.

PLATE 24

# ELEGY IN SEPTEMBER

Solemnly the rain drones its song in the dismal trees,
A trembling brown already waves over the wooded
    mountains.
Friends, the autumn is near, already peering from the woods
    where it lurks;
The field stares, too—it is empty, visited only by birds.
But on the south slope, grapes ripen blue on wooden frames,
Their blessed wombs housing heat and secret consolation.
Soon everything still full of juice, still in sumptuous green,
Will perish pale and freezing, die in fog and snow;
Only the warming wine, the laughing apple on the table,
Will still glow with summer and the brilliance of sunny days.
So too do our senses age, taste the wine of memory
In hesitant winter, grateful for its warming glow,
And from the faded days of parties and joys that have
    fluttered away
Holy shadows wander in silent dance through our hearts,
    like ghosts.

# AT BREMGARTEN CASTLE

Who planted these chestnuts in bygone times,
Who drank once from this old stone fountain,
Who danced in the festooned hall?
They are now gone, forgotten, lost.

Today it is us upon whom the day shines,
Us to whom the dear birds sing:
It is we who sit gathered round tables with candles,
Offering up libations to the eternal Today.

And when we, too, are gone and forgotten,
Still the blackbirds will sing and the wind will sing
In the boughs of the trees, and down below
The river will still froth against the cliffs.

And in the great hall, to the evening cry
Of the peacocks, other people will sit.
They will chat and praise how lovely it is,
And ships with pennants will sail on by,
To the laughter of the eternal Today.

PLATE 25

# NATURAL FORMS

E ven as a small child I had often liked observing bizarre natural forms—not to study and analyze them, but to abandon myself to their unique magic, their confused, deep language. Long lignified tree roots, veins of color in rocks, patches of oil floating on water, cracks in glass: everything like that had cast a powerful spell on me back then, but especially water and fire, smoke, clouds, dust, and, most of all, the spinning spots of color I saw when I closed my eyes.[. . .] I realized that I felt a kind of joy and new strength, a heightened sense of myself, due simply to having stared for a long time into an open flame. It was remarkably comforting and rewarding.

So now, joining the few experiences I had had until then on the path to my life's true purpose, there was a new one. Contemplating such patterns, giving ourselves over to irrational, confused, bizarre natural forms, creates in us a feeling of harmony between our inner selves and the force that willed these patterns into being—before long we even feel tempted to see these patterns as our own moods, our own creations—we see the border between ourselves and nature quiver and melt away and learn what it feels like not to know whether the images on our retina come from external or internal impressions. Nowhere but in these practices can we so quickly and easily discover the extent to which we are creators, how greatly our own soul constantly participates in the continual creation of the world. Or rather it is the same indivisible divinity active in us and in nature, and if the external world were destroyed, any one of us would be able to rebuild it, for mountain and river, tree and leaf, root and blossom, every form in nature has its model and prototype within us and arises from the soul whose essence is eternity, whose nature we do not know but which shows itself primarily as the power to love and the power to create.[...]

The garden no longer smelled sweet, the woods were no longer tempting, the world lay spread out all around me like a clearance sale of old, useless things, boring and unappealing. Books were just paper, music just noise. It was like how an autumn tree sheds its leaves: the tree feels nothing, the rain runs off it, or the sun, or the frost, and the life inside it slowly withdraws into its narrowest, innermost places. It does not die. It waits.

# TREE IN AUTUMN

Still she desperately wrestles with
Cold October nights over her green dress,
My tree. She loves it, she feels bad for it,
She wore it through the cheerful months,
And now she would so love to keep it.

And then another night, another
Raw, cold day. The tree grows weary.
She fights no more; she relaxes, abandons
Her limbs to the force of this other will,
Until it has totally vanquished her.

But now she laughs, red and golden,
And rests deeply happy in the blue.
Since in exhaustion she gave herself up
To death, the autumn, mild autumn, has dressed
Her up in new magnificence.

PLATE 26

# PRUNED OAK

Oh how they've cut you, tree,
How strange and unnatural you look!
How you've suffered, a hundred times over,
Leaving nothing but stubborn will!
I am like you: even in this chopped-up
And tortured life I did not break,
Daily I raise my brow anew,
Through cruelties suffered, toward the light.
Everything soft and tender in me
The world has scorned and mocked to death
But my core is indestructible,
I am satisfied, I am reconciled,
I patiently put forth new leaves
From boughs that have cracked a hundred times,
And in spite of all sorrow I still remain
In love with this crazy mixed-up world.

# A STRAY SON OF THE SOUTH

Outside the rounded arch resting on slim double columns that formed the entrance to the Mariabronn cloister, a chestnut tree stood by the roadside—a stray son of the South brought back ages ago by a pilgrim to Rome. It was a sweet-chestnut tree with a mighty trunk; its full, round crown hung fondly over the path, breathing broadchested in the wind. In spring, when everything around it was green and even the cloister's walnut trees were wearing their reddish young leaves, it kept the world waiting for its own; during the time of the shortest nights, it pushed up through leafy clusters the dull whitish-green rays of its exotic flowers, which smelled so admonishingly, oppressively sharp. In October, after the fruit and wine harvests, the tree's prickly fruits, which didn't ripen every year, would fall from the yellowing crown blowing in the autumn wind, and the cloister boys would scramble and wrestle for them, and Gregor the subprior would roast them in the fireplace in his room. Fondly, exotically, the beautiful tree draped its swaying crown over the cloister entrance—a sensitive, slightly shivering visitor from another clime, related through mysterious hidden channels to the portal's slender sandstone double columns and the ornamental stonework of the window arches, cornices, and pillars so loved by the Latin peoples while the locals gawked and saw them as foreign intruders.

# "DESCRIPTION OF A LANDSCAPE"

I've been living for the past week on the ground floor of a villa in a part of the world entirely new to me—a new landscape, society, and culture for me—and since for now I am all alone in the middle of this new world, and the autumn days in the silence of my new big pretty writing room feel long, I occupy my time by starting the jigsaw puzzle of these notes. It is work of a sort; it gives my solitary, empty days a semblance of meaning; and at least it's an occupation that does the world less harm than the important, high-paying jobs so many other people have.

The place I'm staying is in Switzerland, located very close to the canton boundary and linguistic border, on the French-speaking side. I'm here visiting a friend who's in charge of a sanatorium, and I live right by the edge of this institution, which I will probably get to know better soon under the guidance of the doctor. For now I don't know much about it, only that it's housed in a prodigiously large, castle-like, architecturally splendid building situated on a sprawling plot of land covered with beautiful parks, a former manor.[...]

The spacious sanatorium building, our little villa with two doctor's apartments, and several modern buildings housing the kitchen, washhouse, garages, stalls, and carpenter's and other workshops, plus the nursery with its large plantings, hotbeds, and greenhouses, are in the middle of an extensive park with a magnificent, feudal, and somewhat coquettish character. This park, whose terraces, paths, and stairs slope gently down from the mansion toward the lakeshore, is my environment and my landscape for the time being, since I can't manage longer walks at the moment. The main part of my attention and love is for now devoted to this park. The people who planted it seem to have been motivated by two intentions or, rather, passions: one for a painterly, Romantic division of the space into flat lawns and groups of trees, and another passion to plant and tend, along with the beautiful groups, distinctive individual trees as rare and exotic and striking as possible.

As far as I can tell, this seems to have been the custom on all the estates of the region, and besides, the last owner and inhabitant of this mansion must have brought back a love for exotic plants from South America, where he owned plantations and exported tobacco. Although these two passions, the Romantic and the botanic, occasionally contradict each other and come into conflict, the attempt to reconcile them here has been in some respects a nearly perfect success, and when you wander through the park you find yourself drawn to and pleased by different aspects in turn: now the harmony between plantings and architecture, and the charm of the sudden surprising views and elegant *vedute*, whether out over the breadth of the lake or back at the château's façade; now the individual trees and plants themselves, which entice you with their botanical interest or age or vitality to take a closer look. All this begins right by the manor house, where, on the uppermost, semicircular terrace, a number of southern plants in large tubs are on display, including an orange tree richly hung with plump, glowing little fruits, in no way making the same slight, plaintive, even ill-humored impression that such plants from other latitudes transplanted to a foreign climate usually make. This tree's stoutly teeming trunk, crown pruned into a ball, and little golden fruits seem utterly healthy and content. Not far from it, a little lower down and closer to the shore, we notice a marvelous, vigorous plant, more like a bush than a tree, but rooted in the natural soil, not in a tub, and bearing nearly identical little hard round fruits. It is a strange, thorny plant, intractable and willful, defensively tangled in on itself, impenetrable, with many trunks or stems and many branches, and its fruits are not quite as golden-colored as the dwarf orange tree's. It is an enormous, very old Christ's-thorn. Later, as I keep walking, I will run across others of its kind in various places.

There are some trees related to the yew and the cypress, and alongside them, with an impressive and somewhat bizarre silhouette, is a monkey puzzle tree, alone and maybe a little melancholy but strong and healthy. In its flawless symmetry it is as if lost in a dream, and as a sign that its forced solitude is powerless to harm it, its topmost branch bears a number of heavy, massive fruits. Along with these rarities, intentionally set in isolation on the grass and as it were expressly inviting our attention and admiration, there are also various precious, languorous-seeming trees likewise somehow aware of how interesting they are, slightly robbed of their innocence—weeping willows and weeping birches especially, elegant long-haired princesses from a sentimental age. Though not rare, they have been trans-

formed by the gardener's arts. There is also among them a grotesque weeping pine, whose trunk and all its branches double back from a certain height and reach toward its roots. This bent growth, so contrary to nature, produces a dense hanging canopy, a living pine-hut or pine-cave that a person can walk into, where they can disappear or live like the nymph of this wondrous tree.

Among the most beautiful trees on our sumptuous estate are several gorgeous old cedars, the loveliest of them brushing its topmost branches against the crown of a thick oak, the oldest tree on the property, much older than the park or the building. There are also some thriving sequoias, growing more in breadth than in height, maybe due to the often strong cold winds. For me the most glorious tree in the whole park is not one of the elegant foreigners but a venerable old silver poplar of tremendous height, dividing not far above the ground into two mighty trunks, each of which alone could be the pride of a whole park. At the moment it is still in full leaf, deepening from silver gray through a rich range of brown, yellow, even rosy hues into a heavy dark gray, depending on how the light and wind play upon it, but its colors always have something metallic about them, something brittle and hard. When a strong wind blows through its giant twin crowns and the sky, as sometimes happens in these early November days, is still a

*previous* PLATE 27

wet deep summer blue, or else overcast with dark clouds, it is a regal performance. This venerable tree is worthy of a poet like Rilke, a painter like Corot.

The stylistic ideal of this park is the English model, not the French. The designers wanted to create a supposedly natural, pristine landscape in miniature, and in places this deception is almost a perfect success. But careful consideration of the architecture and the attentive treatment of the terrain and its slope down toward the lake shows in the clearest possible way that we are dealing not with natural growth here but with culture, mind, will, and cultivation, through and through. And I like that the park still expresses all that today. It might possibly be more beautiful if left to itself a bit, neglected, a little unkempt—then grass would grow on the paths and ferns in the cracks of the borders and stone steps; the lawns would be a little mossy, the architectural follies a little sunken; everything would speak of the natural drive toward haphazard propagation and decay; wildness and thoughts of death would be permitted entry into this elegant, beautiful world; you would sometimes see fallen trees, see the corpses and stumps of dead trees overgrown with swampy smaller plants. But there's no hint of any of that here. The strong, precise, doggedly planning human spirit and civilizing urge that originally resulted in the planning and planting of this park still rule over it today, still maintain it and tend to it and leave no place for wildness, slovenly licentiousness, and death. No grass grows on the paths, nor moss on the lawns; the oak is not permitted to reach its crown too far into the neighboring cedar, nor can the trellised vines, dwarf trees, and weeping trees forget their discipline and evade the law according to which they have been shaped, pruned, and bent. And where a tree has fallen and been removed, whether due to illness, age, storm, or the weight of snow, no disorderly place of death and chaotic second growth remains; instead, a newly grafted young tree, small and trim and thin on the old disk, with two or three branches and a few leaves, obediently submits to the order of the place where the fallen tree once was, with a neat strong pole standing next to it, too, to hold and protect it.

Here, in other words, a product of aristocratic culture has been preserved and has lasted into a completely changed time, and the will of the founder, the last estate owner, who donated his property to a charitable organization, is respected and governs even now. The tall oak and cedar obey it, as do the skinny young saplings with their poles; the silhouette of every group of trees obeys it, and a dignified memorial stone in a classical style honors and immortalizes it on the last garden terrace separating a wide lawn from the reedy shore and the water. Even the one visible wound that a brutal age has inflicted upon this beautiful microcosm will soon heal and vanish. During the last war, one of the lawns high on the hill had to be plowed over and turned into arable land. But that empty patch of land is already waiting for rake and harrow to obliterate the crudeness that has intruded there and sow it with grass once again.

Now I've said various things about my lovely park, and yet I've forgotten more than I've described. I owe the maples and chestnuts a hymn of praise, and I've failed to mention the lush, thick-stemmed wisteria in the inner courtyards, and first and foremost I should have paid homage to the wonderful elms, with the one right near my apartment between the villa and the main building being the most beautiful, younger but taller than the venerable oak within. This elm emerges from the earth with a solid thick trunk, but one which, from the beginning, aspires to be tall and slender; after a brief, vigorous running start it sprays apart into a whole population of branches striving toward the sky, like a jet of water dividing into multiple streams—it shoots up, thin, bright, hungry for the light, until its joyful upward movement comes to rest in a high, beautifully domed crown.

Even if there is no room for the wild and primitive in this ordered, cultivated zone, the two realms do collide everywhere along the borders of the park. Even when the park was first planted and laid out, its downward-sloping paths ended in the marshy sand of the flat, reedy lakeshore, and more recently it has much more tangibly been given untamed nature as a neighbor. Some decades ago, due to the digging of canals to connect the region's lakes, the water table of the local lake dropped by five or ten feet, and a wide strip of the former edge of the lake went dry. Since people didn't know what to do with this strip, they let nature take its course there, and now a wood runs rampant, extending for miles, more ragged than the park, a bit stunted, and in places even swampier than the old shore—a jungle of alder, birch, willow, poplar, and other trees, grown from whatever seeds blew over, slowly turning what used to be the sandy lake bottom into a forest floor. An undergrowth of oak is coming up here and there, though it doesn't seem really to feel at home on that soil. And I imagine that various sedges bloom there in summer, silver cottongrass, and the tall orchids with feathered leaves that I know from the swampy fields alongside Lake Constance. This wild growth offers refuge to many kinds of animals, too: besides the ducks and other waterfowl, snipe and curlews, egrets and cormorants nest there; I have seen swans flying; and the day before yesterday I saw two deer walk out of this woods and cross one of the large flat lawns of our park in long, leisurely, playful leaps and bounds.

What I have described here—or if not described, at least summarized in list form: the stately groomed park along with the primitive new woods in the wet new land by the lake—seems like a whole landscape, and yet it is only what lies very close to our house. If I stroll around in this area for a quarter of an hour, up and down the paths, it does indeed form a unity, an enclosed little world; a bit like a park in a big city, it suffices for a while, it makes us happy, and it can stand in for the rest of nature. In reality, though, all of it—park, nursery, orchard, forest belt—is merely foreground, a step leading to something much bigger and more unitary. When you walk the pretty paths down from the house, beneath the tall elms, poplars, and cedars, past the luxuriant cones of the giant sequoias whose thick cinnamon-colored trunks soar up so warm and well hidden behind their tents of elastic hanging boughs, over to the monkey puzzle tree and the smoke tree, the weeping willow and Christ's-thorn, down to the shore, that is when you first face the genuine, eternal landscape whose characteristics are not prettiness and interest but size and greatness: a wide-open, simple, large, immeasurable landscape. Behind the small brownish miniature forest of reeds along the shore, the lake extends for several miles, the color of the sky in calm weather and dark blue-green like glacier ice in stormy weather, and beyond that (when not hidden, as it is on many days, in gray and opal-colored mist), the low, elongated range of the Jura Mountains draws its calm but energetic lines in the sky, and that sky, above this seemingly almost flat expanse, is infinitely large.

## WITHERED LEAF

Every flower longs to be fruit,
Every morning to be night,
Nothing on this earth lasts forever
Except for change, except for flight.

Even the loveliest summer wants
To someday feel autumn, and withering.
So, leaf, stay patiently where you are,
Even as the wind wants to bear you away.

Play out your game, do not fight back,
Let it happen quietly.
Let the wind that breaks you
Carry you back home.

PLATE 28

**PLATE 29**

# BETWEEN THE HOURGLASS
## AND THE WITHERED LEAF

───────────────
❦

A withered leaf blown in through the window, a little leaf from some kind of tree whose name I can't think of, is lying on the edge of my washbasin; I look at it, read the script of its ribs and veins, and breathe in this reminder, so strange, of the impermanence we shudder before, and yet without which nothing would be beautiful. It is marvelous how beauty and death, pleasure and impermanence have each other as prerequisite and consequence! I can clearly feel around me and within me, like something physically tangible, the border between nature and spirit. The way flowers are ephemeral and beautiful while gold is lasting and dull, so too are all the movements of natural life transient and beautiful, while mind and spirit are permanent and wearisome. Right now I reject it—in no way do I see mind and spirit as eternal life, only as eternal death, as petrified, infertile, shapeless, able to take on form and life only at the cost of giving up their immortality. Gold must become flower, must turn into body and soul, in order to live. No, on this warm morning, between the hourglass and the withered leaf, I don't want to hear anything about the spirit, however much I admire it at other times—I want to be ephemeral and fleeting, child and flower.

❦

# IN THE FOG

How strange it is to walk in the fog!
Each solitary bush and stone,
And no tree can see another,
Each one is alone.

My world used to be so full of friends
When my life was still light;
Now that fog has fallen on it,
No one is in sight.

It is a truth: None is wise
Who does not know the dark
That inescapably separates him
From every other creature's eyes.

How strange it is to walk in the fog!
Life is solitary and lone;
No man or woman knows another,
Each one is alone.

# A BROKEN BRANCH CREAKS

Splintered, broken branch,
Still hanging year after year,
It drily creaks its song in the wind,
It has no leaves, no bark.
Bare and pale, tired of too-long
Life, of a too-long death.
How hard the sound, how dogged too,
Stubborn but secretly afraid:
Its song for yet another summer,
Yet another long winter.

# WANDERER IN LATE AUTUMN

Through the tangles of the bare forest's boughs
The first snow falls white in the gray air,
It falls and falls. The world has turned so silent!
No leaf that rustles, no bird in the branches,
Only white and gray and silence, silence.

The wanderer, too, who roamed the green
And colorful months with lute and song,
Has fallen silent, tired of pleasure,
Tired of walking, tired of songs.
He shivers; from the cold gray heights
Sleep wafts toward him, and meanwhile softly,
Softly falls the snow . . .

But memory still speaks from distant
Spring and summer bliss now withered,
Speaks in pale pictures fading out:
Cherry blossoms veiling the blue,
An April-bright, propitious blue—
A young butterfly, brown and gold, hangs on
A grass blade with delicate trembling wings—
From the woods' half-dim wet summer night
A birdsong long drawn out with yearning . . .
The wanderer nods at these dear pictures:

How lovely that was! Still more flutter up
From those former times, flare up and go out:
A sweet dark gaze from a lover's eyes—

A night storm, lightning and wind in the reeds—
An evening flute from a stranger's window,
A jay's shrill shriek in the morning woods . . .
Still it falls and falls, the snow.
The wanderer
Listens for the birdcalls and flutes
That once resounded, stirring his heart:
Oh beautiful world, how quiet you've grown!
Inaudibly he passes through soft white,
Heading home, to his long-forgotten home
Now calling him with gentle urging,
It calls him toward the valley, the alder creek,
The marketplace, the old parental home,
The ivy-covered wall behind which rest
His mother and father and other relatives.

No leaf that rustles, no bird in the branches . . .

# AFTERWORD

*by*

Volker Michels

Hermann Hesse, once he was free to choose where he lived, always lived close to nature, and he had a congenial affinity with the largest, longest-living plants: trees. Losing a tree was for him like losing a friend, and we find described many times over in his observations and books how the loss of a tree can change, can impoverish, our feeling for a place.

Trees were sacred to him, just as they were to our ancestors, not only for their uses and their variety but as allegories of life, symbols of the organic organization of nature. We must take this organization to heart if we are to cope with the challenges of the future, too—challenges the vegetation of our planet face from human civilization, progress, and an increasingly growing population.

Like all living creatures, trees too need light to thrive. As a link between earth and sky, they transform—in the laboratories of their leaves, with the help of the sun's energy—the atmosphere's carbon dioxide into the air that is vital for us and for animals alike, while also contributing to ecological balance with the water tables of the forests. The surface area of the leaves on a large tree, roughly comparable to the area of a soccer field, produces about five tons of oxygen a year. The carbon given off in the process is transformed, in chlorophyll and thanks to roughly eighty gallons of nutrient solution from the roots, into nine pounds of sugar and starch a day. From this arise the substances of a tree's body, such as the cellulose and thus the wood of its trunk, branches, and roots. The tree's stability, like our own, must be ensured by a bond with the earth corresponding to the fullness of its crown. The farther the tree strives up and into the light, the deeper it pushes its roots into the darkness of the earth. In fact, the branching of the root system can be up to three times the branching of the tree's crown. And depending on species and location, trees can anchor themselves in the ground with taproots reaching depths of up to 120 feet (in desert areas) or roots shaped like umbrellas or plates. Trees submit to the whims of whatever they find, even stones or boulders that they can wrap around and cling to. They solidify the topsoil and protect it from erosion, avalanches, rock slides, and landslides.

The flexibility of some tree species, and their resistance to weather and storms, was also exemplary for Hesse—some species that grow up to 320 feet high, like the sequoia or the Chinese dawn redwood, can withstand even fire and cyclones so well that structural engineers use their example to try to discover the laws of stability and weather resistance. Other scientists study how we might improve our pumps based on the absorbency of tree roots, since trees like the eucalyptus and coastal sequoia can bring water and nutrients ten times as high as our conventional suction machines. Because nature has so much more knowledge than we do, we can only learn from the intelligence of evolution. That is why our human technology, whether on land, on water, or in the air, is more efficient and more aesthetically beautiful the more precisely it follows the precepts of nature.

Especially in his early stories, Hesse liked to describe the magic of the woods of his Black Forest childhood, the play of light in the vault of the treetops, the smell of buds in the spring, the columnar great halls of fir trees, and later the lush sweet-chestnut slopes of his adopted home in Ticino. Forests, apart from these sensuous qualities, are for us today necessary filters for pollutants, since up to fifty tons a year of dirt, acid, soot, and carbon dioxide are absorbed by a single hectare of woods.

The individualist in Hesse also honored trees that stood alone, in a different way from how he respected whole forests. In the essay "Trees," he compared such trees to great solitary human beings "like Beethoven or Nietzsche. The world rustles in their uppermost branches, their roots rest in the infinite, but they do not lose themselves in either, they work with all the strength of their lives toward just one thing: fulfilling their own law that lives within them, shaping their own form, becoming their own selves. A tree says: The attempt the eternal Mother made with me, the risk She took, is unique—my shape is unique, the grain of my skin, the tiniest play of leaves on my crown and the tiniest scar on my bark. My task is to give shape to the eternal, and to show that shape in its unique, distinctive particularity."

This passage appears in the hymn to trees where Hesse laid out his core beliefs on the subject. It was written shortly after the First World War, after he too had struggled to defy the turbulence of those years and preserve his honor with appeals to international humanity, even at the cost of being smeared as a "traitor to the fatherland." These attacks on his independent spirit didn't leave him unscathed—neither the attempts to break his will when he was a boy, nor the defamations of the war years. And so he is describing himself, too, when he says about the sight of a sawed-off tree trunk, "in its annual rings and deformities are faithfully recorded all the struggle, all the suffering and illness, all the joy and flourishing, the lean years and rich years, attacks withstood and storms outlasted. And every farm boy knows that the hardest, noblest wood has the narrowest rings, and that the most indestructible, strongest, most exemplary trunks grow high in the mountains, in constant danger." For the dead heartwood inside a tree, up to ninety percent of its substance, is like an archive, passing down centuries' worth of living conditions. Wrapped in the growth of the living sapwood layer, the tree dies as it grows, just as we do. Here, too, annual death is in service of life that continues nonetheless from year to year.

It is no accident that Hesse titled one of his books of poetry *From the Tree of Life*, words taken from the first line of the poem called "Transience": "I feel leaf after leaf falling from the tree of life." The poem dates from 1919, from the turnaround after the war, during which Hesse experienced more than just a stylistic new beginning in his creative work. As he confidently remarked in a letter written around the same time, "I hope I will put out new leaves for a few more summers, and so rustle in the wind whether or not the trunk is still young. I want to make all sorts of music, in my way, and I look forward to it, only my view of that future is often obstructed by clouds." Thus trees for him were also emblems of a development he could accept and welcome, for it involved constant regeneration. You might think, during the winter, when a tree is robbed of its magnificent canopy of leaves and looks frozen and dead, that all is lost, yet that same tree reawakens to new life every spring. Many kinds of trees and bushes, in fact, have such powerful "élan vital" that they start to bloom even before their leaves appear, as if reproduction and progeny were more important to them than what sustains their own life. Hesse's hymn to trees touches on that, too: "My power is trust. I know nothing about my fathers, I know nothing about the thousand children I produce every year. I live out the mystery of my seed to the very end—that is my only concern."

There is also Hesse's delight in the multiplicity of nature's inexhaustibly different shapes and forms—the rich diversity of species, the construction of trunks and crowns of branches, the shapes and placement of leaves, the structures of bark—while mankind today is ever more inclined to standardization and flattening. He answered a reader's letter in 1955 by saying that "tree" is satisfactory as a concept, "but our body and soul can't do anything with 'tree.'" What they need and love are: linden, oak, sycamore." With regard to the leveling of different religions, he added, "If God expresses Himself differently in India or China than He does in Greece, that is not a flaw or lack, it is richness; if you want to summarize all these different ways the divine appears with a single concept, you won't get an oak or a chestnut, but at best a 'tree.'"

The same way nature expresses itself in its plants, trees, forests, and meadows, humanity does with its buildings, settlements, and cities, which are more beautiful and more organic the more they adapt to and integrate the surrounding vegetation. As a result, Hesse saw treeless, congested urban areas as lacking in character—places as interchangeable in memory as train stations. Amid the hectic life of our cities, trees for Hesse were like monuments to slowness and forbearance. For he saw patience as "the most difficult thing, the only thing that is worth learning. All of nature, all growth, all peace, all flourishing and beauty in the world relies on patience—it takes time, quiet, trust, faith in long-term things and processes that last much longer than a single life," as well as faith in the interconnection of things, including ones we don't yet know about. Since trees live longer than we do, thereby linking us with future generations, he concluded one of his poems about the chestnut trees in the courtyard of Bremgarten Castle above the Aare River with these lines:

*And when we, too, are gone and forgotten,*
*Still the blackbirds will sing and the wind will sing*
*In the boughs of the trees, and down below*
*The river will still froth against the cliffs.*

*And in the great hall, to the evening cry*
*Of the peacocks, other people will sit.*
*They will chat and praise how lovely it is,*
*And ships with pennants will sail on by,*
*To the laughter of the eternal Today.*

# SOURCES

The following dates of writing and publication, and the location of the original texts in Hesse's Complete Works (*Sämtliche Werke*, ed. Volker Michels, 20 vols. [Frankfurt: Suhrkamp, 2001–07], citations by volume and page number), are taken from the German edition of *Trees*, with places of first publication and details about revision and newspaper versus book publication omitted. Titles followed by an asterisk were supplied by the German editor, Volker Michels, for untitled poems or excerpts from longer works.

"TREES": Written 1918. First published March 10, 1919. XI:20–21.

"MY HEART GREETS YOU"*: Written April 1896; originally untitled. X:435.

"GOOD FRIDAY": Written April 4, 1931. X:313–14.

"THE OLD COPPER BEECH"*: First published April 1905. VI:363–65.

"MOVEMENT AND STILLNESS IN HARMONY"*: First published April 29, 1952. XII:588–91.

"FLOWERING BRANCH": Written February 14, 1913. X:188.

"THE MIRACLE OF REBIRTH"*: First published August 1904. VI:192–93.

"SPRING NIGHT": Written May 1902. X:132.

"CHESTNUT TREES": Written 1904. First published April 2, 1906. XIII:37–42.

"DREAM": Written August–September 1901. X:108.

"THE PEACH TREE": First published March 10, 1945. XIV:193–96.

"IN FULL FLOWER": Written April 10, 1918. X:236–37.

"HERMITS AND WARRIORS"*: From *Peter Camenzind* (1904). II:8.

"SHACKLED POWER AND PASSION"*: Written Autumn 1906. First published 1907. VI:547–48.

"THE BIRCH": Written January 1900. X:57–58.

"MAY IN THE CHESTNUT FOREST": First published May 12, 1927. XIV:26–30.

"THE BLACK FOREST": Written 1901. X:75.

"TREES": Poem by Joyce Kilmer (1913).

"UPROOTED"*: First published July 1913. VIII:82–83.

"PAGE FROM A DIARY": Written April 1939. X:358–59.

"LINDEN BLOSSOMS": Written 1906. First published 1907. XIII:148–51.

"LAMENT FOR AN OLD TREE": First published October 16, 1927. XIV:48–52.

"VAGRANT HOSTEL": Written August 1901. X:88–89.

"OPPOSITES": First published July 9, 1928. XIV:99–104.

"NIGHT WITH MOUNTAIN WIND": Written February 13, 1938. X:355–56.

"THE LITTLE PATH": Written 1919. First published April 1921. XIII:403–06.

"SUMMER AFTERNOON AT AN OLD COUNTRY HOUSE": Written June 24, 1941. X:367.

"ELEGY IN SEPTEMBER": Written September 1913. X:188.

"AT BREMGARTEN CASTLE": Written August 14, 1944. X:373.

"NATURAL FORMS"*: From *Demian* (1919). III:316 and 286.

"TREE IN AUTUMN": Written 1904. X:166.

"PRUNED OAK": Written July 1919. X:269.

"A STRAY SON OF THE SOUTH"*: Opening paragraph of *Narcissus and Goldmund* (1930). IV:271.

"FROM 'DESCRIPTION OF A LANDSCAPE'": Written November 1946. First published March 1947. XIV:201–07.

"WITHERED LEAF": Written August 24, 1933. X:324.

"BETWEEN THE HOURGLASS AND THE WITHERED LEAF"*: Written 1923. XI:56–57.

"IN THE FOG": Written November 1905. X:136–37.

"A BROKEN BRANCH CREAKS": Written August 1–8, 1962. X:398.

"WANDERER IN LATE AUTUMN": Written September 1956. X:387–88.

# LIST OF PLATES

**HERMANN HESSE** was born in 1877 in Calw, Germany. He rose to become a celebrated author and the recipient of the Nobel Prize in Literature in 1946. As the son of missionaries, he developed a fascination with self-discovery and spiritual explorations, an interest also likely due in part to his lifelong struggle with depression, which led him to study Sigmund Freud and, later, to undergo psychoanalysis with Carl Jung. In 1912 he moved to Switzerland, where he wrote his best-known books, including the classic *Siddhartha*; composed poetry; and

*continued*

painted landscapes. He passed away in 1962 in Montagnola, Switzerland. Hesse is one of the most widely translated authors of the twentieth century; his work continues to have influence worldwide.

**VOLKER MICHELS** is primarily known for his work as an editor at the Frankfurt publishing house Suhrkamp Verlag (which later expanded to include Insel Verlag). There, his focus from 1969 to 2008 was to make the works of Hermann Hesse more accessible and to advance the Nobel laureate's literary and artistic legacy; this included editing the first complete edition of his writings, consisting of approximately fifteen thousand pages in twenty volumes. Michels is the world's foremost authority on Hesse's work and also manages his literary and artistic estate.

**DAMION SEARLS** is a writer and the translator of fifty books from German, Norwegian, French, and Dutch, including Hermann Hesse's *Demian*; he also edited a one-volume abridgment of Henry David Thoreau's journal. His own books include *The Inkblots*, a history of the Rorschach test and biography of its creator, and *The Philosophy of Translation* (forthcoming). He has received Guggenheim, Cullman Center, and National Endowment for the Arts Fellowships, as well as the Helen and Kurt Wolff Translator's Prize for Uwe Johnson's four-volume novel *Anniversaries*.